Cup O'Joy
and a fresh taste of the bread of heaven

....

Elle Waterhouse

*To Josephine —
May God bless you richly —
Blessings!
Elle Waterhouse*

Cup O'Joy
*and a fresh taste of
the bread of heaven*

Copyright © 2016 by Elle Waterhouse

All rights reserved. No part of this book may be reproduced or transmitted in any form or by any means without written permission from the author.

ISBN: 978-0-9913270-6-5

E.P.I.C. Publishing Services LLC
www.epicpublish.com

Just A Word?

I have been thinking about the impact that words have. They flood our ears and manipulate our emotions. The right word at the right time can be an almost magical entity; whereas cutting phrases aimed with razor sharp precision wound so many of us. I cannot buy into the thought that words are just words. I am a writer and that may have something to do with it; but there is more at stake than that. Words have power.

Scriptures say much about our use of words. The book of Genesis talks about how God spoke and creation came into being. Believers are encouraged, exhorted, and warned about the use and misuse of speech in everyday life. The way that we use words matters to God and to others around us. It makes a difference when we use speech to encourage each other instead of throwing insults to buffer our pride. It makes a difference when we pray for the irritating people that we live with in our daily lives.

I will share what I believe that Scripture has to say about the matter. His words are life to us. In light of that truth, I pray that the Lord blesses my efforts at relaying what I believe He has laid on my heart.

Elle Waterhouse

Sing

Sing to the savior now
For His redeeming grace

Sing to the savior now-
His grace
Is just a prayer away.

For His hand is sure
And He knows my frame-
And glory rests
On His throne

His hand comes down
And pulls me up
To gaze on fields of white...

So I sing to my Savior now
For His redeeming grace;
I sing
For His love renews
The spirit placed within me
For His name.

Rising Up

Rising up;
ready to put on the garment of praise...
fiesty, I am;
gearing up to do battle; preparing to fight off
person, place, or memory....
Rising up;
assured of His willingness to rescue my cause
for the sake of His glory;
Rising up;
knowing past reason that His paths
are laced with that bittersweet balm
flowing down from the mercy seat.
Rising up;
raising my hands in defiant praise
as I strain to ignore emotion's pull.
Rising up;
determined to trust in my Lord as our hands
meet once more on the journey.

Mental Deposits

The weather is turning warmer and I can feel the serotonin levels in my brain rising with each passing day. That is a wonderful thing. I haven't written much these days; on account of finding work. Yes, I am working full-time right now and spend my days depositing my energy into the tasks set before me there. In honor of the impending season of SPRING, I am going to celebrate in the face of working so much. In short, I choose joy.

My mental deposits for the moment are a whirl of meandering sentences and phrases sitting in a holding cell. SPRING has snuck out of the enclosed area and burst forth in my consciousness with a renewed spunk. Snow is going to have to wait until a colder month to come back for a visit.

What are your mental deposits for the day? Mine were a tad quirky today (so feel free to be silly if you are so moved).

White Space

In the white space
of Genesis -
Before the story
of the formation
Of the universe...
There was God-
Infinite being
and creative force...
Reaching out
to call forth
Matter
To assemble
According to
Willful design...
In the beginning
There was God-
And He was good...

Spoken

The Spoken Word
was released
and went forth;
creating earth and sky...
...and water...
...and man...
Creation's glory
reflecting the eternal majesty of the Father...
Even when the universe
had yet to behold earth's creation,
I wonder at the conversations held among
the trinity's members;
amazed at the care and the forethought
conceived and brought forth
with the spoken Word...

Walking on the Wire

Taking on the day
that the Lord has made,
I try to rejoice and be glad.
My brain is full of messages and replaying images
vying for my focus and cluttering my thoughts.
Turning to the Lord in entreaty and faith,
it seems I am walking on the wire between faith and anguish.
Double-minded walking... the thought
pierces me and brings me low.
He is worthy to receive honor,
worthy to receive praise,
and yet I am walking on the wire between
faith, trust, and white-knuckle tension.
I look beneath the wire I see in my mind
and see the grass below looming as a
ravenous lion in a den-like cave...

A hand pulls my head up to focus on Jesus,
and His eyes bring me back to the knowing
of grace...
to trust in His mercy
I will just have to trust Him,
and moment by moment relinquish my all.

Casting my Cares

Casting my cares
On the Lord;
Faith arises in me-
Sensing that
He will
Indeed
Sustain me!
Moment by moment
I'm trusting
And praising;
Resting in Him
And strengthened
By His joy.

Song on the Breeze

There's a song on the breeze
Sent from the Savior's hand;
Calling me home to His heart.
The cares of this life
Pass with the fading mist-
Over the waters of my days...
For I know that I know
His love endures forever-
Bringing out the praises
From my soul...
The garment of praise
Descends
From the Spirit's hand-
Lifting the heaviness
From weary bones.

Clouds

The heavens declare the glory of God; And the firmament shows His handiwork.
~Psalm 19:1

I've taken it to heart to study the clouds as of late. The crisp edges and the darker corners of these vaporous formations enthrall me. They rise up to the heavens; bringing our gaze upwards towards the One who created them as a natural part of human existence.

Clouds have been instruments of divine guidance (way back in Genesis), Rorschach tests between human psyche unwilling to leak the contents of their soul to mortal agents, and wonderful distractions. The unreachable canvas of the sky holds its' majestic inhabitants in parading costume. They are not usually controlled by human interventions (i.e. cloud seeding).

I imagine while I am watching the clouds that God has an extraordinary sense of beauty and its' importance to the human psyche. I can further imagine that their temporal beauty is only outdone by the eternal beauty that rests beyond our sight. I cannot imagine the beauty of heaven. Mercy does not permit me to gaze upon realms of glory while my body is still among the material of earth. Watching the clouds gives me a miniscule taste of that glory; and for the moment I am satisfied.

Enjoy the clouds and linger to send up a prayer for His presence in your life. Mentally send your concerns on the air in the middle of those vaporous creations; allowing His hand to reach where mortal reasoning cannot...

Intercession

"So I sought for a man among them who would make a wall, and stand in the gap before me on behalf of the land, that I should not destroy it, but I found none."
~Ezekiel 22:30

Looking out on the sea's mist,
my spirit drawn to dancing with a soft cloak;
the faces come into my memory
and bid me
kneel my spirit's will towards
the dew of heaven......
the arms of Jesus
hold each one
in tender reverie...
proclaiming grace and Word
as hedges against erosions of faith
within human form;
and bringing back
the peace past conscious knowing
to rest upon and

heal
each
furrowed
brow.

A Sweet Conversation

I say, "Good Morning" to the Lord
and wait for His reply...
thinking how elaborate and deep
His response will be...

"Good morning, Lynne"
is what I hear...followed by
"I love you"

He is not what I expect sometimes,
and infinitely more...
as practical as dew and sun;
He knows my frame
and considers the finite
capacity of my understanding.

Mercy He shows to me
who does need it;
awaiting instruction and
yearning for fellowship

with the One who speaks to
my deepest parts
...from the vantage point of eternity...

Sweet conversation from deep unto deep;
flowing through time
and yet up-to-the-minute...
details attended to with soft
nudging pokes;
and vision renewed in the light of His glory.

He Is My Joy

He is my joy in the morning,
showing me the love that endures
in ways my speech cannot convey to mortal
ear.

He is my joy through my day's journey;
sustaining the breath within me
by the grace and mercy flowing from the
cross.

He quiets me with His love as I lay
down upon my bed;
dispelling the fear that looms to steal His joy
from my grasp;
and singing His love song to me as I dream
of the vineyards.

Up

Up from the ashes;
my soul arises to praise His name...
words unable to express
what spirit to spirit can communicate
without words...
Up from the bed of mourning
to lift up holy hands
in thanksgiving for His tender mercies...
knowing that beauty for ashes is
His glorious promise;
grace and love
wrapped up in His sacrifice;
stretching on towards eternity's shores...

Baby Steps

I am sitting at the computer tonight wondering if I have anything to contribute. I don't consider it writer's block; as there is so much in my heart that is pounding at the gates to burst forth in full gallop. Rather, I wonder if what I will say will be of much blessing or merit. I suppose the issue at hand is my confidence meter. The magnet in this proverbial compass is bouncing from end to end as a bobble head at a town fair.

I have heard it said that every journey begins with a step. Baby steps. Tentative forays into what will become the future. If we think too long about each step instead of just stepping out in faith; then paralysis sets in to immobilize us. Impulsive leaps can give us battle scars as we try to climb out of the morass we create for ourselves. Humanity interacting with itself is a mess.

This is the day that the Lord has made. I will choose to rejoice and be glad in it. If the best I can do is capture the joy between tears; then that is a valid place to start. Each redirected thought focused on all that is pure and lovely will leave its mark; like a notch in a mountain meant for the climber's boot.

Baby steps....let's hear it for the days of small beginnings that lie ahead for all of us. We can raise our glasses of living water and celebrate the joy that lies ahead. Past the veil of the present; it awaits us as we step out in faith and walk towards the sound of His voice.

Letting the Rocks Cry Out

Sister, don't let the rocks cry out
before you stand with hands raised up to praise Him!
Sister, don't let the rocks cry out;
letting those things without the breath of God within them
offer up their sacrifices of praise...

Brother, don't let the rocks cry out
before you offer up thanksgivng
for His mercies!
Brother, don't let the rocks cry out;
withholding the garlands of praise from Him
who created the heavens and the earth with words;
the strength of His Spirit propelling the elements into action...

Children, don't let the rocks cry out
before you sing together of His marvelous love!
Children, don't let the rocks cry out;
letting the sound of the praises
in your heart to escape;
inviting Him to inhabit your praises;
knowing that where Love is there is peace past human comprehension...

Shine

Shine your light
from heaven's shores;
illuminating my ways;
allowing me to push past
the veil of earth's misguided trust
in all that is but temporal...

Cast the net
and catch me, Lord;
though as fish go
I won't be much...
dispel the cloak descending
with a touch...a word...
or an angel with skin on.

Restore the years
that locusts have eaten;
devouring the wheat
and polluting the wind...
until I arise from the bed of my mourning
to joyfully share of Your unchanging love.

Greetings and Salutations

I am writing this with a wiggly bi-pedal life form on my lap. She is three, so that explains why she is on my lap and wiggling. I am also in the process of trying to catch my breath. My mind is swimming; and I shall have to catch a thought or two as they fly by the white spaces.

Today is the day that the Lord has made.
Today is the day that the Lord has made.
Today is the day that the Lord has made.

I am holding onto that verse as a lifeline. He has everything under control. I do not. Life is a fly-by-the-seat-of-my-pants adventure; especially these days. I could not have imagined what He has done and what He will do. When He gets ready to do His thing, events can move pretty fast.

I rejoice in my relationships today. I am so thankful that my efforts at coming out of the creative closet have met with such generous support. I am doing what I was born to do; and there is not doubt in my mind. He does His thing and I do mine; and hopefully they become one on a regular basis!

I pray that you rejoice in this day; regardless of circumstance.

He's got your back...

Mercy's Reign

Mercy's reign
comes down with grace;
enfolding us in the arms
of God
for the sake of His glory...

Mercy's reign
takes the lead in the struggle;
allowing His love to
raise high the hands of praise to His name.

He reigns in majesty;
allowing us glimpses of future glory,
and bringing His voice
to the spirit of man...

Flight

Up from the grave,
He arose with healing in His wings;
breaking the teeth of sin and death
with the triumph of new life...
and can you imagine the rejoicing in heaven
when a new soul discovers His joy?
He paints the seeking soul with mercy's flow;
binding up the wounds,
breaking free the embattled spirit bound in the
clay of earth...
Up from the grave,
that one sacrifice provided the path to life;
once and for all,
offered with the love that knows no limit
as understood by the finite understanding of
human flesh...
Up from the grave,
His glory renews us;
fulfilling the promise and prophecy.

Nahum 1:7

The Lord is good,
A stronghold in the day of trouble;
And He knows those who trust in Him.

I came across this verse in Nahum this morning. Like many scriptures, there is much to be read and understood between the lines. Memories and those Spirit whispers flood my mind as I read this verse; bathing the verses with a sustaining power only available in the realm of faith.

"The Lord is good". Oh, yes. He is good. He is past good and all the way to great in ways my flesh cannot fathom. Thank God I cannot see everything ahead of me. He knows better than that; and that the end result would be a straight jacket! His goodness is amazing. How can we imagine everything that he has ahead for us? How can we imagine the many ways that he works things out on our behalf? He is glorified in heaven with, I am sure; the most sublime melodies. Yes, He is good; and we are at His feet for His mercy and grace because we know that He is good.

I am thankful that He is my stronghold in those times of turmoil. What other hope do I have; save the exploding mercy of my God? He knows that I am dependent upon Him for His provision and grace. He even created within me that desire to fellowship with Him; making every substitution weak and pale in comparison to the joy of His presence. He knows my heart, and yet still desires fellowship with me. Right there is the edge of my understanding. Beyond that, I have to just trust that He knows what is best.

My prayer is that I can discern His voice and follow with a whole-hog abandon that will show me His plans for my days. May he cleanse my lenses to allow a clear picture of who He is in the days to come.

Near to Me

You are near, O Lord,
And all your commandments are truth.
~ Psalm 119:151 (NKJV)

You are near;
regardless of my level
of knowing...
Beyond my finite comprehension;
Your ways envelop me;
surrounding me as a hedge of protection.
Morning finds me raising my hands
as hands that reach towards heaven
wait for You to meet me
where I am...
You are near;
seeking me
while I am seeking You;
seeking me
while I am looking towards
hazy horizons
and often in the wrong direction...
Still You are near

The Hand

*In the Lord's hand is the life of every
creature and the breath of all mankind.*
~ Job 12:10

In His hand,
paths are made straight;
allowing grace
and mercy
to intersect at the points of need...
for in His hand,
the mystery of just...being...
offers a richness and joy
infused within the gift of breath.

He Makes Me Wait

My strength,
song,
and everlasting joy;
He makes me wait.
Sometimes in the green pastures,
sometimes in the arid places
which seem bereft of water or comfort...
yet He is faithful to provide for my needs
according to His riches in Christ Jesus...
He is my fortress,
deliverer,
and gracious Father.
Sustaining life and bringing joy,
often when I figure that
I have gone past the reach of grace...
yet in Him I live,
I move,
and I have my being....
and my praises shall arise
to the throne of heaven.

Sure-Footed

One thing I have desired of the Lord,
That I will seek:
That I may dwell in the house of the Lord.
~ Psalm 27:4-6

All the days of my life,
To behold the beauty of the Lord,
And to inquire in His temple.
For in the time of trouble
He shall hide me in His Pavilion;
In the secret place of His tabernacle
He shall hide me;
He shall set me high upon a rock.
And now my head shall be lifted up
above my enemies all
around me;
Therefore I will offer sacrifices of
joy in His tabernacle;
I will sing, yes, I will sing praises to the Lord.

Renewal

He takes my hand
and walks along;
providing solace
and sweet fellowship.
The steps begin
as tentative forays
into the land of the unknown;
yet become sure;
purposeful declarations
of trust in a faithful God.
I feel the sand beneath my feet;
massaging the flesh
and cooling the roughened edges.
Gradually, the earth becomes firm;
transforming into polished granite...
His words and whispers
taking my soul and spirit
towards glorious renewal.

Brewing

Direct my steps by Your word,
And let no iniquity have dominion over me.
~ Psalm 119:133

Just brewing, thinking, of what You said;
letting the rain fall,
wet and then soak the soil of my soul;
waiting in anticipation for the seed to burrow down,
germinate and push through the soil in victory;
knowing that the words will produce fruit
in the physical realm.
Holding the image of the fruit yet to come,
I wait in anticipation of sharing the fruit;
knowing by whisper and past paths
how the joy grows when the fruit is shared
on the family table.

A Sweet Conversation

I say, "Good Morning" to the Lord
and wait for His reply...
thinking how elaborate and deep
His response will be...

"Good morning, Lynne"
is what I hear...followed by
"I love you"

He is not what I expect sometimes,
and infinitely more...
as practical as dew and sun;
He knows my frame
and considers the finite
capacity of my understanding.

Mercy He shows to me
who does need it;
awaiting instruction and
yearning for fellowship

with the One who speaks to
my deepest parts
...from the vantage point of eternity...

Sweet conversation from deep unto deep;
flowing through time
and yet up-to-the-minute...
details attended to with soft
nudging pokes;
and vision renewed in the light of His glory.

New Mercies

My manifesto for the day will include scriptures on trust, grace, mercy, and anything else that I can cram into my gray matter. I am determined to rejoice today at home, at work, and in transit to...wherever. Yes, I know that His mercies are new every morning. It is also true that I am told by His Word to give thanks in everything. I can do this. Yes, I can. Philippians tells me that I can do all things through Christ who strengthens me. Good news...no...Great news. My feet of clay will not melt today.

Now where did I put that...perspective? I know I had it for a while yesterday. Did I put it in...no...it isn't there. Could I have tucked it away for safekeeping? It must have been an absent-minded moment where I just put it down anywhere. I know where my keys are, and that is a start. However, I seem to have misplaced my perspective. I need it. Let me look one more place ...yes...no...yes...no ... and I think I have found it. You are not going to believe where I had it tucked away.

My perspective was tossed out by an outburst of emotion. I am reduced to a two-year old melting down because mom told me "no". Somehow I had begun to reason that if I just kept pulling God's ear to resolve the issue at hand he would get tired of hearing my whining and just do as I was telling him. Fresh, huh? Yup. That is why I needed my perspective. God is still God. He knows my end from my beginning. He renews His mercy and compassion every morning. It is morning. I have a fresh batch just waiting for me; and I am hungry. I think that is how it is supposed to be. I will seek Him; and He will find me.

Sailing and Wading

It's always something.
Each day has its' troubles;
enough to juggle between hands,
nose, feet, knees, and the unseen flutter
of angels' wings...
Either sailing or wading;
the continual struggle to
offer up the sacrifice of praise in the midst
of the wilderness...
and even in the greener pastures;
memories of darker shadows
propel us to our knees in search of Jesus' ear...
Oh, Lord, it is always something;
molding us with fire and confounding circumstance.
It's always something, but there is always...You.

Closer than a Breath

Just a prayer away;
His presence
comes and rests;
upon the care-strewn landscape
of our souls...
He makes a way
where we cannot see the path;
knowing that our frame
is sustained by His grace
...and His mercy
woven into the fabric of our days...

I was talking to my mom this morning. Caregiving is taking a toll on her; and she just takes it day by day. There was little I could say in consolation except to remind her that the Lord is only a prayer away; and closer even than a breath.

Running Ahead...

Running ahead of You,
I left you in the dust...
convinced in my mind that I knew best;
attacked by temporary insanity?
Now I am asking You to bless my mess...
knowing that You alone know where to start;
and confident that You are able
to configure glory out of
my trail of disobedience.

Morning Song

Looking up towards heaven,
this is the day that the Lord has made...
yet the new day with all of its' promise
retains vestiges of what clings and stings
from yesterday...

"My mercies are new every morning," I can hear my Lord say;
yet the fog of emotion pulls me back
to the land of regret and anxiety.
I try to cast my care on Him,
but the fishing pole at my side
seems to hold onto whatever I attempt to cast.
I feel the care speed back to the depths of my soul...

"My grace is sufficient" adds the Spirit with patience,
knowing my frame is a package of dust and

Spirit.
"fearfully and wonderfully made"
as my Lord tells it...
and I choose to believe Him over whatever other source
attempts to convince...

Lord, this is the day that You have made.
Help me to rejoice and be glad in
the work of your hands...
for I know that I know that Your love
endures forever;
awaiting my confessions of failures and fears...

Take my hand today, Lord, as every day...
and hold tightly as I step out in faith;
knowing that Your grace is sufficient for my needs...
and that You are everything I need to survive.

Looking Up

I'm standing here, Lord;
knowing past reason that You are near.
Looking up towards the heavens
and all that You have made;
the music of heaven wells up
from the depths of my soul
to loosen the toughened roots of bitterness.
Looking up brings me down to level
needed to lay my sacrifice at the altar.
I'm standing here, Lord;
knowing past reason that You are near
as I seek Your heart.

From the East to the West

As far as the east
is from the west,
You have taken our sins...
...confessed, forgotten, and
completely removed
from your memory.
We puzzle You,
I do suppose,
when we remind you
and re-submit
our petitions for forgiveness
to Your throne.
"What's this?"
I can hear You say...
"I have already granted
your request, and
you are forgiven.
Take my forgiveness
and taste of my rest."

The Wind

Soft cloak of purple enveloping;
carried on the wind
in a whisper...

speaking to my heart
in thoughts of
majesty for His name's sake.

enduring love
peeling back layers of
black and
dross-covered Band-Aids
self-applied
with weak adhesive...

fresh air infusing
the lungs of body and spirit;
pushing the fog to the side
with new life.

Finally, brethren, whatever is true, whatever is honorable, whatever is just, whatever is pure, whatever is lovely, whatever is gracious, if there is any excellence, if there is anything worthy of praise, think about these things. What you have learned and received and heard and seen in me, do; and the God of peace will be with you.
~Philippians 4: 8 & 9

Whatever is True

Whatever is true,
whatever is noble;
purpose my heart, Lord,
to think on these things...
releasing to You
those mental curmudgeons
obscuring the view of that glorious day.
Whatever is lovely, Lord,
I pray to get fixed on...
grounded in joy
and buoyed by grace...
For You, Lord, are truth;
and transforming to beauty
the ashes I hold in my hiding place.

Perception

I am still brewing in my spirit over Joe's message yesterday. It seemed as though the Lord was accessing my mental archives and whispering directions to me as I sat and listened. He had me by the ears; gently holding me in place so that He could reach my heart. I love how He does that. My prayer for today is that I will not run ahead of Him; but allow His leading to bring me to where His perfect will would have me to be...

Perspective?

I've heard it said that perception is everything. Pithy half-truth aside; I think that depends on the mental clarity and the health of perspective that exists. Lenses get filthy and obscure the true picture of any given situation. Perception is powerful; yet cannot hope to encompass the big picture.

Human perception is a malleable entity. Cultural, socio-economic and psychological distortions seem to conspire together (to obscure a compressive view and/or assessment of a problem). It is amazing to me the lengths that human personality will go in order to rationalize its' behavior. A transient perception can propel us towards far-reaching consequences. Perception can act as a betrayer of truth.

Perception. What a concept to consider; and how like a chameleon it can change. We justify our behavior because we perceive that our stated position is as gospel to the faithful! The heart unredeemed and not looking through the lens of eternity is painfully unable to pull itself out of deception's grasp.

We need the promise of redemption's glory to renew our hope; to renew our hope that our perception can be rescued. Seeing ourselves as we are; and yet seeing that we are still sought after in love and entreaty adjusts our perception. Our Lord can adjust our focus and understanding in order to heal our perception; enabling faith to buoy us in our Father's hands.

It's Always Something

The title of this is a familiar phrase to many of us. It either precedes or follows the relating of some recent hardship or startling event to somehow soften the blow it inflicted. The truth contained in it was brought home to me once more as I listened to the message in church yesterday. My pastor was talking about the lessons we can learn from Abraham and Lot all the way back in the book of Genesis. As he was talking of how God is the same God He was back then, I felt a hearty "Amen" rising in my spirit.

Between the cradle and the grave, there is always something to challenge us, provoke our sense of adventure, or smack us in the face with our feelings of inadequacy. Yeah, it can be rough to be human. The good news is that the Lord knows this from personal experience. He spent time in an earthsuit. Sure, He was God incarnate; but also had the physical experience of life down here with us.

Like many folks, I am often stuck at various points between "Thank God" and "Oh, Lord...just shoot me now!". Offering up my sacrifice of praise in these moments is a loftier goal that what I reach some days. Still, He tells us that His mercies are new every morning. Good thing. I need some more of that mercy to cover me with His grace. God has much work to do in me. Those feisty spots of self-will and mini volcanoes need a special touch; as the impact is often felt by those around me. He doesn't honor those flash prayers of "beam me up, Lord!" In light of that cold fact, I am forced to remain and seek His will and presence while there is daylight.

I pray that you are enveloped in His peace today as you deal with your own "somethings."

Evening

Taken off the shelf
dusty with age,
It's rainy autumn outside
inviting her to open me,
My verses read silently,
savored slowly,
the words and the pictures exposed to the outside world.
Life springs up in all of its' glory,
inspired by love and sustained by My grace.
My words make an inventory, a picture, and whispers
leading my reader along in My presence
along the pathways of peace.

In Remembrance

My heart is full tonight. I have a relative visiting in the area; and a joyful reunion took place earlier today. We had the chance to visit. She had the opportunity to meet my children. We saw memories and felt connections with each other formed over years of fellowship. I even think we look in each other's faces and see traces of those who have gone before us to be with Jesus. I am brought to remembrance of so many things that have fashioned our lives; and yet only one has held us together over the years.

There is something rapturous about being with other believers. Family for me is synonymous with Christian fellowship. Conversations around the chowder pot on the fourth of July were not about the popular culture. They were about sharing our lives and discussing the joy of knowing

Jesus. We lived in remembrance of Him; listening to each other and hearing the Spirit whisper to us between the lines...

I can't help but think of all the verses in the Scriptures that talk of praise. "Praise the Lord" is a much-repeated phrase. Thanking God for His tender heart and rejoicing in His promises are themes that drench the reader of so many verses. In Malachi 3:16, "Then those who feared the Lord spoke to one another, And the Lord listened and heard them; So a book of remembrance was written before Him

For those who fear the Lord and who meditate on His name".(NKJV). My grandmother used to have a plaque on her wall that spoke of Christ being a silent listener in every conversation. I can still remember reading those words every time I went with my mom to visit my grandmother. Rich soil was cultivated by the power of those words.

In closing, I will feel my spirit reach out to the Lord in entreaty and longing. Those who have gone before me see clearly the beauty of the Lord in all of His majesty. I have to wait to see them again and to enter that praise fest. Those who remain after me will have to be satisfied with photo albums, birthday cards, and the retelling of "old times" they remember while I was still with them. It will be a small part of the Lord's reflection; but a compelling foretaste of the glory to come.

Reflections on 2007 Art 4 the HEart posts

I joined the Art4HEart fellowship this spring; happy to find an outlet for a closet obsession. Writing is many things to me: an act of worship, a creative outlet, and a second nature exercise that brings me much joy. The fellowship of others with the creative bent has been amazing; and I count it among my highest joys of 2007. I am in my element; and yet basking in the glow of His presence.

I would look at the offerings of my fellow bloggers and see amazing examples of photographic praise and linguistic flow. I was green with envy over what I saw them posting; and that is why I didn't share much of what I would write before then. What I wrote was for me; to burn or to create without commentary or criticism.

An amazing thing began to happen when I began sharing what I write: others responded with positive encouragement. They saw value in what I would offer; and receive blessing from it as well. Go figure...

I was soon offering what I would have previously either ignored or written incognito and shoved under an out-of-the-way book. It has been my joy to share what the Lord gives me. He has given me so much through my association with the artist's fellowship: friends, an outlet for my passion, and a newfound joy in being who He made me to be.

I am only one of a talented group of artistic folk at our church. Bill and Liz have their photos and the insightful text that accompanies them. Janet takes the ordinary and infuses it with a touch of the divine;

while David, Christa, Judy, and Phil often speak of beauty and commitment to the cause of Christ with a joy and a clarity that shines. Diane, Nancy, and Masha do not post; but are always willing to bless us with what the Lord gives to them.

I am thankful that there has been an opportunity to praise God; and allow a forum for a group of creative people to offer up what the Lord gives them as an expression meant for the body of Christ as a whole.

December Fades

Short days
follow crisp winds;
reflections on the soul's waters
bring shadows of memory,
lights of discovery,
and clarified goals...
December fades into the winter paths
of January...
leaving behind the celebration
of the Christmas glory.

Living and Powerful

For the word of God is living and powerful, and sharper than any two-edged sword, piercing even to the division of soul and spirit, and of joints and marrow, and is a discerner of the thoughts and intents of the heart.
~ Hebrews 4:12

Reading Your words,
I am exposed...
flesh and soul
sliced open simultaneously
with precision and grace.
Alive and powerful
...and, oh, yes...sharp;
moving past pretension,
denial, and rationalization;
releasing pressure
and draining infection.
Sweet rain falls down;
rehydrating the arid patches

and lifting my spirit towards
that sweet fellowship in the Spirit...
Reading to find You;
so that I can find me....

Singin' and Swingin'

Singin' and Swingin'
and getting merry like Christmas;
I'm getting the hang of this praisin' thang...
Glory surrounds me
as the song in my heart grows;
carving out nooks for the Spirit
...and washing my spirit
in mercy and grace...
Singin' and Swingin'
as a statement of faith
as I am caught between the now and the "not yet"
that I am so longing for...

In offering up a "sacrifice of praise" to the Lord, I have found sweet rest for my soul. I can hardly wrap my brain around how He does what He does to renew us and work all things out for our good. Thank God I don't have to figure it out. I just need to learn to trust Him with my pieces; and He will make me whole again.

Hebrews 13:15-16
Matthew 6:33-34
Proverbs 16:3

Jubilant Faces

Joy in the morning
now 24/7;
each soul knowing each other
as unending light permeates
every corner;
prompting the ready praises
in glorious music;
continually singing in celebration of His presence.

Joy in the morning
and all the day long;
showing on faces once known
for their illness and sorrow...
now raising their voices
towards the face of Jesus;
reveling in the presence of God
as they all enjoy fellowship
and unending grace.

Bright Eyes Shining in Smoke

Bright eyes glistening,
raised towards the Way and the Life,
Smoke from the day's burnt offerings
obscuring the rays of light from heaven.
Sweet water to quench what burns within me;
the strains of sweet salvation's inner music,
gentle whispers float
and settle upon the good soil
turned up,
churned up from the passing tempests.
Bright eyes still glistening and waiting on the Lord
as smoke gives way to
burning sun,
warmth,
and the promises of eternity.
Love is renewed out of the remembrance of Your faithfulness.

Lifeline

I will not fear
and open doors
for cold invasions
to leave me bereft of comfort
and left for dead...
I know You're there, Lord...
Oh, tell me why I've felt the icy grip
refusing to release me
from its grasp...
I believe, Lord,
Help me to latch on to the lifeboats
clapping the surface
of the water next to the docks...
Those pictures I will not speak of with words...
relying on the depths to give up their dead
and release the living from the grasp of descending night...
I call on You...
O precious Jesus

knowing you came to seek and to save
those who are lost...
and place my hand in Yours for my rescue.

Soft Light

I write, Lord, and You speak to me...
"deep unto deep" as You say in Your word...

The footsteps I have heard
in distant walks have left footprints in the soft earth;
giving pause to time warp passages
...and illuminating my path ahead...

You speak and sometimes I strain to hear
over mental static and outer distractions...
...the familiar yearning to sit with open Word
and pour out words onto a page...

Fresh vision You give
and breezes to cool the coals
as the dross burns and brands my memory...
knowing that the journey ends with new
hope and ongoing words of restoration...

Therefore Choose Life

Guilt repelled off
the armor provided,
designed to protect the creature of clay;
soul soil entrusted into the hands of the Lord...
choosing life...
choosing joy...
over stubborn refusal
to chew through the restraints of the enemy...
enticed by distorted desires within...
for the chewing produces
strength of spirit...
galvanizing resolve to seek clarity of perception...
choosing life...
choosing joy over the piercing familiarity of the abyss.

Sound Bite

He hears the cry for mercy,
though there has been no word...
or tear shed to otherwise indicate
soul distress...

He takes the thoughts held captive
in holding tanks of mental junk...
-infusing new vision and sweet balm of
heaven
to heal the spirit's wounds of one still
trapped in feet of clay...

Colors of the deepest blue
relay from heart to heart...
lightening from near black to a royal hue...
the Spirit's hug is reaching in
...to heal and walk along to safely guide
His creation to the shore...for deep waters
are no hindrance
to the One who made the seas...

The scars are there
...with whispers of molded clay
calling out to the potter for further molding
...and a hoped for restoration to
what cannot be fathomed this side of
Glory...

The inward eyes cannot turn away from their presence,
as the flesh of the scars hold diamonds and jewels
...and a promise of beauty for ashes to yearn for...

Identity formed with image unfolding;
grace poured into the vessel of earth...
assurance of company
in midst of fog and soft cloak enfolding;
familiar perception now questioned with bated breath...
...a comma where a period had been before...

Battle Cry

The hand
drew back the covering veil;
exposing the warrior swords
clashing with the talons of dark shadows;
The Spirit's whisper floated in the air;
bringing prayers
brought by the sons and daughters of the promise;
jew and gentile
joining together to lift up the battle cry
for the deliverance of the promise.

New
He will create a heart that's new
among the brambled mass
of past attempts
at being "strong" apart from
embracing arms.

The stretch of His arms

loosened the grace;
given through the blood;
the river of life...
pouring over flesh to
cover the sins of the world.

This day retains the joy that came
when death turned into life...
a resurrection in our hearts
of His eternal life...

The bride of Christ we'll be that day;
shimmering in the realm of glory;
without spot or human wrinkle;
no foible to shortchange the stores of heaven.

Joy of heaven,
stuff of earth;
divine touching mortal;
glory's flame opened up the path to
heaven's portal...

Little Billy

"A man's gotta do
what a man's gotta do!"
He proclaimed
for the ears
of those he wanted to impress.
All 5 years and 30 lbs. of him
occupying
space and time
in purpose
and awareness
of life on the horizon's distant handshake?
He had to do
what he had to do-
reaching forth into time
to declare
his faith in what would emerge as truth.

Potholes and Banana Peels

It happened. I slipped.

That besetting sin snuck into my being and
    put the banana peel on my path.
    I fell. It hurt.
The pothole I fell into was dark and damp.
I could feel the chill of darkness creep into my bones
    and bring with it that familiar ache.
I should have known better than to play with the images;
    should have known that the end would be smelling of death.

    My old fascination with potholes and b-skins had
    conspired with evil to bring me down low...

    and actually watch the old pictures of grim windows
    show me what evil would have me

become.

Now I have to get myself out of my pothole.

My digging in mire has brought me to naught

but regret and a fog-walking

into the realm that I have known for so long.

I finally remember the call of the savior to

seek and to save that what was lost,

and cast my sins into the sea of the forgotten

as an outpouring of love and His grace.

"Jesus! I need you to touch me and heal me; for you

are the One whom my heart longs to reach.

Just the hem of your garment brought healing to one...

but You are near me, and speaking of grace.

My Lord and my savior,
Be near me today.

The Knot

Psalm 94:19, Psalm 46, Philippians 4: 6 & 7

The knot arose
with stealth
and vigor;
gripping the corners
of my stomach
in increasing measure-
catching the thought
and taking it captive-
I laid it down upon the altar
and
prayed for the fingers
to release me
from captivity-
then...breathing deeply...
and entering into the rest of the beloved.

Declaration

I will wait on You, Lord-
Set my course
towards
a path of courage
for the sake
of your glory-
Then I will see Your hand
to the left
and to the right;
rejoicing as You renew
and strengthen my mind;
restoring my soul;
I will wait on You, Lord;
For You alone
are where
my soul
will
find
rest.

Promise

Isaiah 40: Reflection

I feel the soil
    beneath my feet
as my spirit
    tries to rest
in the presence of God-
writing in
    a mental notebook,
my heart pours forth
    longing and desire
        to draw near
wind blows
    and sun shines
through
    the daily path,
whispering to me
of the promise
    available at the foot of the cross.

Painting

He paints across my soul;
Colors of flesh and purple;
Tracing the cracks and broken corners
With grace and mercy's brush;..
The hand appears and the fingertips
go over
the arid patches with a soft touch...
Transforming what seemed dead
into a vessel of beauty.
I see Him through tears of thankfulness;
Standing near with eyes full of love...
And then He paints again to draw His picture;
And my soul aches with the beauty of the colors
and the light interwoven with great care
and forethought...
I gaze and see the joy burst forth
from the darkness.

Crawl

Crawling onto the altar exhausted;
I had been fighting my battles
with paper swords
        and deferred hope;
Then sensing the warmth of His love;
"fear" became "fearfully and wonderfully
made"...
The words and phrases of life
became emblazoned upon my paper sword;
Melting together on the surface
and transforming my weapon
into a blade of steel and fresh hope;
Lifting the spirit within me
to arise and walk.

or...

Crawling onto the altar exhausted;
I had been fighting my battles with paper
swords

and deferred hope;
Then sensing the warmth of His love;
the words and phrases of life became
emblazoned upon my paper sword,
transforming it into steel;
enabling me to arise and walk.

Possibilities

It is possible
to see His paintbrush
gliding across
the canvas of our time-
It is possible
to rest;:
Seeing the beauty painted
from our ashes
Come alive
as His Spirit moves among the brethren.

If I Wait

If I wait;
If I hope in You
and embrace
the strength and courage
found in Your presence;
You will strengthen me
and lead me in Your ways.

Looking

I will look for You, Lord;
Shifting my gaze
away from the transient flies
which land upon my nose.
I will set my eyes
on the intricacies
of Your creation;
pushing behind the design
to find the designer;
I will search in anticipation;
knowing that You can be found
when there is room in my spirit.

Praising

I will praise You;
knowing that You
are worthy of
my praise-
I will praise You;
trusting that
You are always
on time-
More than able to meet
our needs
according to Your riches in Christ Jesus

Wherever You Go

Where You go-
Lord, I want to follow-
Yearning to draw near
And let Your fire
burn off
The dross around me;
Just enough light
for the next step-
Replenishing my spirit
And bringing new measures
Of blessing in the valley

Finding Joy

Those who love Your name
Can be joyful, Lord;
As You are able
to do
what (with us) is impossible!
They shall run with endurance
The race set before them;
as Your presence
Brings life, healing,
And an abundance of joy. A Prayer for You

Beyond

Past the Holy of Holies;
liquid joy compels me
to raise my hands
in submission and praise to the Lord.
Past the Holy of Holies;
peace, joy, and healing descend
and restore the broken pieces in my spirit
as I drink in the liquid joy again.

Teach Me

Teach me how to wait, Lord-
pushing away
mental cobwebs
to approach the shore of truth;
I'm waiting on You, Lord,
and expecting You to
grant me courage
to walk with You again.

Discovery

I'm learning,
leaning,
enjoying the view...
knowing that I can depend
upon the strength of your tender mercies...

I'm rejoicing in sorrows;
releasing my burdens into the hands
of One who knows that my frame is...dust...

You've known my ways
and see past the blinders I cling to;
even when I run into walls
by refusing to take them off...

You've treasured my voice
as I've come before you in pained entreaty...
drawing me to Your heart
as I look for Your face in the melee of circumstance.

You've held me close
and listened patiently
as myopia shaded Your hand from my view...
knowing that I would be rewarded for
my longing for Your truth to be made known to me...

If I Wait

If I wait,
If I hope in You;
and embrace
the strength and courage
found in Your presence-
You will strengthen me
and lead me in Your ways.

(Psalm 31:24)

Poem

Snatching
Words and phrases
From
Mental soup;
My words become
A part of someone else
As they emerge
From
The innocent pen.

Able

He is able-
To create something new;
able to revive neglected embers
with perfect timing
and abundant mercy.
He is able
to renew the Spirit's fire
within the confines of an earthen vessel,
and beyond the realm of human comprehension.
He is able
to sustain the flame
amid the assaults thrown forth;
aware of blessings
waiting on the other side of the mountain.
He is able...
And He is enough.

I was thinking about those verses in the Scriptures that speak of the act of praising God. Offering up a sacrifice of praise seems to invite the Spirit of God into our circumstance. My meager understanding was enough to pull a few words out of my spirit and through the keyboard of the computer. May He bring you to a place of praise for your benefit as well as for His glory.

Sacrifice of Praise

The sacrifice of praise
arose from the ashes;
scenting the offering's remnants.
Joy had come in the morning;
growing from the bile grown in
the gardens of self-seeking...
Act of will and sound of weeping
coming together to offer
the sacrifice of praise
until the emotion caught up
with the act of faith.

A Prayer for You

May our Lord
Remain as your strength
and refuge-
And may His love
repel the shadows of fear
increasing your sense of wonder...
to lead you to be still
and know that
He
   is
      your
         God.

About the Author

Elle Waterhouse writes in the seat of domestic bliss as a wife and mother; she is also the pet parent to a couple of furry friends.

Elle puts pen to paper for the fun and encouragement as an act of celebration. Active in church life, she enjoys being a part of a worship team.